World Première

A comedy

Charles Mander

Samuel French—London
New York-Toronto-Hollywood

CHARACTERS

Members of the Whickam Amateur Dramatic Society (WADS):

Val, the prompt; young
Sonia, the Leading Lady, some years older than Val
Stuart, slightly over the hill Leading Man
Gordon Truelove, ageing Producer and Playwright
Ruth Truelove, Character Lady and wife of Gordon

Other characters:
Arnold Brisket (Lanes and Hedgerows); late middle age
Mrs Partridge (Mothers Union), middle age

The action of the play takes place on the stage and in the auditorium of the South Westbury Church Hall

Time—the present

WORLD PREMIÈRE

The stage and auditorium of the South Westbury Chuch Hall

When the CURTAIN *rises, the stage, shabby and bare except for curtains, is in darkness. Sonia, elegant and slightly petulant, is sitting in the stalls. A shaft of light appears off* L

Val, a small indeterminate young woman clutching a plastic shopping bag, enters

Val (*fumbling her way on to the stage*) It's dark. Hallo?
Sonia Hallo?
Val Who's that?
Sonia It's me.
Val Oh ... Ruth?
Sonia (*briskly*) Certainly not!
Val You're not the caretaker, are you?
Sonia No, I am not the caretaker.
Val Ah ... Sonia?
Sonia Correct.
Val Are you in the hall?
Sonia The auditorium ... Yes.
Val In the dark?
Sonia Seemingly.
Val Ah ... I suppose ...
Sonia If you are going to ask why I am sitting in the dark it is because I can't find the bloody light switch.
Val Oh.

Gordon, an ageing, failed professional actor and now long-time producer of the Whickam Amateur Dramatic Society (WADS), enters the auditorium

Gordon (*blundering in*) Blast!
Val What?
Gordon (*bellowing*) Lights! Lights!
Sonia We can't find the switch.
Val Pardon?
Sonia I said ...
Gordon Who's that?
Sonia Oh, God!

Stuart enters. He is a civil servant and romantic lead, slightly over the hill, who never stops acting on or off the stage

Stuart (*from the stage*) What's the problem?
Gordon Lights! Lights!
Sonia Lights!
Val Er ...

The Lights come up

Ah.

Gordon is advancing through the auditorium

Stuart And the Lord said, Let there be light and there was light ... Brilliant.
Sonia It was God, actually.
Stuart What?
Sonia It was God who said let there be light. You're paraphrasing again.
Stuart I never paraphrase.
Sonia What? You never paraphrase?
Stuart Never. I am always completely word perfect ... well, nearly always.
Sonia You weren't word perfect in *The Farmer's Wife*. You paraphrased so much you changed the plot.
Stuart Would it have mattered?
Sonia Well, maybe not to you but it did to the rest of the cast who were thrown into utter confusion and the prompt into hysterics.

Gordon Where's the set?
Stuart Good heavens ... the set ... (*looking round*) It's not here.
Gordon What's the time?
Val Er — just coming up to three, Gordon.
Gordon Well where the hell is it? We're supposed to have a
technical rehearsal at three. We've only got sixty minutes, they
only allow us sixty minutes.
Val Shall I go and look for them?
Gordon (*sharply*) Stay where you are. I don't want anyone
wandering off. I know what happens when people wander off,
they completely disappear. All of you stay here and do something.
Sonia Do what?
Gordon Rehearse.

Gordon hurries out

Stuart Another cock-up. No set and half the cast missing, par for
the course.
Val There's some chairs out there, I'll bring them in and then we
can practise a bit.

Val bustles out

Sonia (*shouting after her*) Rehearse, rehearse. This is a theatre, not
a golf course.
Stuart Theatre? (*He looks round*) You must be joking.
Sonia I am speaking metaphorically.
Stuart Yes, luvvie.
Sonia (*dangerously*) Don't luvvie me, Stuart. I've bitten legs off
better men than you!
Stuart I bet you have.

Val enters dragging two chairs

Val Here we are, now we can sit down.
Sonia So we can.

Sonia sits in one chair and Stuart sits in the other

Val Oh ... Yes ...

Val trots out in search of another chair

Sonia That woman fawns ...

Stuart I bet they're bonking in a layby ...

Sonia She fawns about Gordon and everybody else hoping to get a part. But she'll never get a part because she's new, can't act, and hasn't the first idea ...

Stuart Since when has being able to act been a performance criterion in this group?

Sonia She can't even prompt efficiently. Usually about three pages behind and when she does give you something it's useless and you can't hear it anyway.

Stuart Well, it doesn't matter then, does it? If it's wrong and you can't hear it. It doesn't matter.

Sonia It doesn't matter to you because you never say anything remotely resembling the script. I'm surprised Gordon hasn't shot himself or you — which would be a better idea.

Stuart I bet they're bonking somewhere.

Sonia Who?

Stuart Damion and that bimbo from the fish shop. I don't know why Gordon let them do the stage-management.

Sonia She is not a bimbo, her name is Sandra and she is a young woman.

Stuart Oh yes — all right, all right ...

Sonia And Damion is an oversexed bastard.

Stuart Oh, really? Has he had a go at you, Sonia?

Sonia Mind your own business.

Stuart (*laughing*) My God, I bet he was short-changed there. Did you fell him with a karate blow?

Sonia Just shut-up, Stuart, or I might fell you. I have no time for male chauvinist pigs!

Val enters dragging in a large throne-like chair

Val This is all I could find. It's rather heavy.

Stuart Great. (*He transfers to the throne. Declaiming*) Attend the lords of France, Normandy, Leicester ...

Sonia Burgundy, Gloucester. You can't even get that right.

Stuart Does it matter ... Does it bloody well matter?

Sonia Yes, it does. If you are going to show off by quoting King Lear you might as well quote correctly.

Gordon enters agitatedly from the wings

Gordon Are you rehearsing?

Stuart Yes ... *King Lear.*

Gordon Who?

Stuart *King Lear* ... Attend the lords of France, Burgundy, Leicester.

Sonia Gloucester.

Gordon I wish you'd stop fooling about, Stuart. You're quite good when you put your mind to it. But you're always fooling about.

Gordon sits in the remaining chair just as Val is about to do the same

Val Oh, sorry, Gordon ... I'll — I'll ...

Val goes off the other side questing for another chair

Gordon I can't find anybody. I can't even find my wife.

Stuart Have you looked in the pub?

Gordon That's not funny, Stuart. If you know what I have to put up with, it's not very funny.

Stuart No ... I meant for the others. The, er, Committee or whatever. The scenery.

Gordon They should be here. Everybody should be here. (*He looks round and notices that Val is not there*) Now where's she got to?

Stuart Who?

Gordon That woman ... Val ... the prompt. I told her to stay put, where the hell has she gone?

Sonia Questing for chairs.

Gordon What?

Sonia She is collecting chairs from various parts of the theatre and depositing them here. You are sitting on one of them.

Gordon We don't want chairs. We want the set and the technicians and the stage director and ...

Val enters backwards dragging in a battered settee

What on earth are you doing?

Val Er — setting.

Gordon Setting what?

Val Well, chairs — and things.

Gordon Strike them.

Val Pardon?

Gordon Strike them. Take them away, lose them.

Val But ——

Gordon We can't get the set up if the stage is cluttered with chairs and thrones and settees. Get rid of them.

Val Oh — all right, then. (*She struggles with the settee*)

Gordon And don't go away. I'm going to have a look in the pub. (*He starts to go*)

Stuart I'll come with you.

Gordon No! Stay here. Please stay here.

Stuart What's the point? We can't do anything ...

Gordon If you go away you'll disappear and then someone else will come and they'll disappear and then you will come back and there will be nobody here and you'll disappear again. Disappearing is endemic in this outfit.

Gordon disappears

Stuart I think he's getting too old for Festival work.

Sonia Yes ... but you have to admit there is a certain confused logic in what he said. I think this must be the most hopelessly amateur and uncommitted company that I have had the misfortune to be a member of.

Stuart Well, we haven't all been to drama school, luvvie, but we
do our best not to knock into the furniture.

Sonia (*dangerously*) It's a bloody pity you haven't been to drama
school. You might have learned some discipline.

Stuart Yes, ma'am ... very good, ma'am. (*He salutes extravagantly*)

Val Excuse me.

Sonia (*snapping*) What?

Val I can't move this settee. I think it's come off its castors.

Sonia Oh, leave it!

Val But Gordon said to clear the stage ...

Sonia Leave it! For goodness sake sit down. You're making us
restless with your coming and going.

Val Oh ... but you see ——

Sonia Littering the stage with chairs. Give it a rest, Val. Sit down
and stop fiddling about. There's not going to be a rehearsal
anyway. We haven't got a set.

Stuart It's being bonked in on the A38.

Val I beg your pardon?

Stuart Nothing ... (*Declaiming*) Meantime, we shall express our
darker purpose ...

Val What?

Sonia He's misquoting from *King Lear*. Oh, God, this is a bore. I
don't know why the hell we bother.

Val gives up and perches on the recalcitrant settee

Stuart Because we love it, ducky. (*Singing*) Hi tiddle ti tee an
actor's life for me. (*He prances about*) You walk about with a big
cigar, it makes no difference where you are ...

Sonia I mean it wouldn't be so bad if we had a decent play and a
decent director. Gordon's past it. Been past it for years.

Stuart (*leaping and dancing*) Hi tiddle ti tee ...

Sonia Oh, for God's sake, Stuart ... (*Shouting*) STUART!

Stuart What?

Sonia You're giving me a headache.

Stuart (*ceasing*) Sorry, just sharpening up the song and dance. Might need it in the future.

Sonia Well, sharpen it up somewhere else.

Val I thought it was rather good ...

Stuart Did you? I can do monologues as well, you know ... there's a little green-eyed idol to the south of Kathmandu ...

Sonia Oh Christ! (*She stands up*)

Stuart Where are you going, petal?

Sonia Away from you ... to get a bit of peace.

Stuart But I love you, petal, you are my favourite man eater.

Sonia Get stuffed!

Sonia stalks out

Stuart Wow! Fire and brimstone. Methinks she's in a tizzy.

Val Did she really go to drama school?

Stuart Oh yes ... Sonia went to drama school and don't we know it. (*He looks round lecherously twirling an imaginary moustache*) Alone, forsooth ... (*He advances upon her, leering*)

Val I think I should put the chairs and things away.

Stuart You're new, aren't you?

Val Yes ... this is my first time.

Stuart But you have been warned.

Val Warned?

Stuart About me. My reputation. Completely untrue, utter calumny.

Val Oh ... yes ... I'm sure.

Stuart However, I admit that I am strangely attractive to the opposite sex.

Val Really?

Stuart Well ... sometimes ... I mean ——

Val Excuse me ...

Val picks up both chairs and bolts past him

Stuart Ah well ... You win some, you lose some. What made you join our little group, Val. An irresistible desire to tread the boards?

Val (*off*) Pardon?

Stuart Do you long to perform?

Val returns and drags off the throne

Val (*off*) Oh no. I mean I don't think I could do that ...
Stuart Prefer to work behind the scenes, eh?
Val (*off*) Yes ... work behind the scenes ...
Stuart Makes a change.

Val returns

Val Change?
Stuart To the others. They all want to act. The only trouble is that half of them can't. And those who can go to the operatic.
Val I thought you had to be able to sing to join the operatic. (*She starts pushing at the settee*)
Stuart Good God, no. If that were the case they'd be down to about three members. If you can sing, you join the choral, if you have a modicum of acting talent you join the operatic. If you can't do anything you join this mob ... Welcome.
Val Oh dear, that's a bit ... er ...
Stuart Cynical?
Val Well ... yes ... a bit cynical.
Stuart If you had been suffering under the uncertain direction of Gordon Truelove for as long as I have, you'd be cynical.
Val Oh ... I wonder if — er — you could help me with this settee? (*She tugs and heaves at it with considerable energy*)
Stuart That man's got a mind like a demented grasshopper. Changes his moves at every damned rehearsal. You don't know whether you're coming and going. Two of us ended up trying to sit on the same chair in one production. And he's over the hill ——

The settee suddenly comes unstuck and shoots into the wings with Val attached

Val Oh, heavens!

There is a thump and clatter

(*Off*) Ahhh!

Stuart — ought to have been put out to pasture ten years ago ——

Val (*off, in a throttled voice*) I say ...

Stuart — and Ruth with him. He's clapped out and she's a dedicated drunk. They make a right pair.

Val (*off*) Excuse me. I'm trapped ... could you?

Stuart It wouldn't be so bad if he didn't believe he was a playwright as well and make us all perform in this utter twaddle. (*He brandishes the script*) He does it every year, you know. Thinks he's bloody Harold Pinter. (*He quotes the title*) "Going Backwards Down a Well" by Gordon Truelove — meaningless self-indulgent crap. I tell you, if it hadn't been for a strong sense of loyalty, I'd have been in the operatic long ago.

Val (*off*) Help!

Stuart (*dancing and parlandoing in an exaggerated voice*) The rains in Spain lay mainly in the plain ... Tarrara ra ra ... (*noticing at last that Val has disappeared*) Hallo?

Val (*off*) Help!

Stuart What?

Val (*off*) Help! I think I'm trapped.

Stuart (*looking about*) Where are you?

Val (*off*) Here ... under the settee .. something fell on me.

Stuart Oh, for God's sake ...

Stuart goes out. Gordon rushes in

Gordon They went straight past me. Nearly ran me over ... (*Coming up short*) Oh no! (*He rushes downstage and peers into the auditorium*) Are you there?

Stuart (*off*) Lift up your leg so I can grab hold of it.

Gordon Pardon?

Val (*off*) Oh! Oh! please don't rip my skirt.

Gordon (*looking round*) Who's that?

Stuart (*off*) Never mind your skirt, just lift your leg ...

There is a thump and a little yelp from Val

(*Off*) Got it! Now just relax.

There is a series of grunts and gasps

Gordon What on earth? (*He peers into the wings*)
Stuart (*off*) Hallo.
Gordon Oh no, Stuart. Not here ... please don't do that here ... we're
   supposed to be having a technical.

Stuart emerges supporting a dishevelled Val

Stuart Val got assaulted by the settee.
Gordon (*following them in, not convinced*) The settee? Oh, really?
Stuart Yes, really.
Val I was trying to pull it off and it ran into the fire extinguisher.
Gordon I didn't want it off. Why have you taken everything away.
Stuart Because you told her to.
Gordon Nonsense. I need the furniture for the rehearsal. You'd
   better bring it all back.
Stuart I wish you'd make up your mind.
Val I think I'm going to faint ...
Gordon Please don't do it here. Really, Stuart, you should try and
   control yourself for once.

Stuart drops Val, who sinks to the floor

Stuart What?
Gordon You know very well what I mean.
Stuart Let's get this straight, shall we? Let's get this straight.
Gordon Well, it has happened before. Remember *Daisy Pulls It
   Off*?
Stuart Oh, that.
Gordon She did, didn't she? In the downstairs dressing-room right
   in the middle of act one and you both missed your entrances.
Stuart (*simply*) I didn't.

Gordon Don't be disgusting. Honestly, you can be really disgusting ... (*Seeing Val*) Why is she lying on the floor?

Stuart Probably fainted. I do that to women. It's always the same. Get a chair ...

Gordon (*hovering*) What?

Stuart Get a chair.

Gordon shuffles off

(*Kneeling, slapping Val's cheek*) Come on, wake up, Val.

Val Where am I?

Stuart Here.

Val Oh ... (*sitting up*) Did I faint?

Stuart Apparently ...

Val So sorry ... I — er ... I'm rather given to it, I'm afraid. Awful nuisance. So sorry.

Stuart No problem.

Val Shock — whenever I get a shock I faint.

Stuart Just like that?

Val Just like that. The doctor says its psychosomatic. Stupid, isn't it?

Stuart Well, it could be a bit of a hazard if you're prompting for this group. There tends to be a shock a page.

Gordon returns

Gordon Damion and that girl nearly ran me over. God knows where they think they're going with the set. I suppose you haven't seen Ruth. I forgot to look in the pub. What with sets whizzing by and ——

Stuart You were going to get a chair.

Gordon Was I — why?

Stuart Because Val fainted, that's why.

Gordon Oh ... yes, of course. I knew there was something. Don't go away.

Gordon hurries out

Stuart I think Gordon's becoming mentally challenged. You've got nice legs, Val. Very nice legs. (*He pus his hand on Val's thigh*)

Val (*springing up*) I'm all right now, thank you.

Stuart (*sprawling backwards*) Hey — steady on.

Val Oh ... sorry — er ...

Stuart (*declaiming in a dying voice*) I am dead, Horatio. Wretched queen, adieu ... Urrrgh!

Val Oh ... very good — er— very good. (*She giggles nervously*)

Gordon returns with a chair

Gordon Here ... oh ... I thought ... (*To Val*) Did you faint?

Val Er — yes.

Gordon Then why's he lying on the floor?

Stuart I cannot live and hear the news from England!

Gordon Well who wants the chair, then?

Stuart (*getting up*) Nobody, I don't know why you brought it in.

Gordon But .. Oh, I give up. (*He sits on the chair, sunk in gloom*)

Stuart What are we going to do?

Gordon Eh?

Stuart Are we going to rehearse? Are we going to sit about examining our navels, or play whist or what?

Gordon I don't know — I honestly don't know. I have been damned nearly run down by that idiot Damion, tearing past the theatre with the set. Ruth has done a runner. There appears to be nobody here in charge of anything. Sonia has vanished and all I'm left with is you and a fainting prompt.

Stuart Could it be, by some slim chance, that we have arrived at the wrong venue?

Gordon Certainly not! I know you may think so, but I am not that much of a fool. This is North Westbury, I take it?

Stuart Presumably.

Gordon Well that's what it said up the road. It said North Westbury welcomes careful drivers. That's what it said, I think.

Stuart Did it? I suppose that is why Damion passed through in such a hurry.

Gordon Don't be funny, Stuart. (*He fishes about in his pocket and produces a crumpled bit of paper*) There — you see. Whickam Drama Society Technical Rehearsal, North Westbury Parish Hall, 3 p.m. This is North Westbury, we are in the parish hall and it is after 3 p.m.

Stuart So where is everybody?

Gordon I don't know — I don't know. It's probably that stupid Margery woman, the so-called organizer, forgotten to tell the management. Useless, that whole damned committee's utterly useless, if you ask me. I mean fancy having an important festival in this place. A world première ...

Stuart A what?

Gordon This play ... My play is a world première.

Stuart Oh, is that what it is?

Gordon Yes.

Stuart Ah.

Val, having fully recovered, now starts bringing the chairs back

Gordon (*to Val*) What are you doing?

Val Pardon?

Gordon What are you doing with all those chairs?

Val I — er ... I'm setting the stage.

Gordon Why?

Stuart Because you told her to.

Gordon Did I?

Stuart Yes, you did.

Gordon I suppose we'd better rehearse.

Stuart Who with?

Gordon Oh.

Ruth, a faded beauty, totters in to the auditorium, somewhat the worse for wear

Ruth Hallo, luvvies.

Gordon Oh, no!

Stuart Ruth, darling. Where have you been? Gordon's been looking for you.

Ruth I got lost, darling, and found myself in a pub.

Stuart Good heavens — how awful.

Gordon (*beating his hands together in despair*) That's all I need! That's all I need! (*He sinks back into the chair overcome*)

Ruth Give me a hand up, duckie ... I'm a bit wobbly on my pins.

Stuart By the gods I will, madam, or else lie in the grave.

Stuart prances down and scoops Ruth on to the stage

Come my Hippolyta, what cheer my love. (*He flourishes extravagantly*)

Ruth (*giggling*) Silly boy. Help me to a chair will you. I am not in the best of health.

Gordon Well you've chosen a very good time for it, that's all I can say.

Ruth Just a stiffener, duckie. Need to brace up, you see, on account of this drivel we all have to perform in. (*She laughs immoderately*)

Gordon Are you referring to my play?

Ruth Awful twaddle, darling. Like all the others.

Gordon (*indignantly*) What!

Val Er — I wonder ——

Gordon Shut up!

Val But I ——

Gordon Clear the stage.

Val But ——

Gordon Put everything back. I'm sick of being mucked about and having my work slandered. I give my all for this company, I drive myself into the ground. The play's off. I'm going home and I shall probably taken an overdose of sleeping pills.

Gordon stalks off in a tizzy

Stuart That's done it.

Ruth Oh dear, poor Piglet. Another tantrum. Did I· upset him?

Stuart I think you did, duckie. How you two have managed to remain married for all these years beats me. I'll go and pacify him.

Ruth Couldn't we all go to the pub instead?

Stuart No, we're supposed to be having a technical rehearsal, or had you forgotten?

Ruth Oh, that. So where's the scenery?

Stuart It appears to have passed us by ... Val?

Val Yes, Stuart.

Stuart (*quietly*) Keep an eye on Ruth. I'm going to talk to Gordon.

Val Oh — er ...

Stuart goes

Ruth (*suspiciously*) Who are you?

Val Er — Val.

Ruth I'm Ruth.

Val Yes — I know.

Ruth You know? Are you psychic?

Val I'm the prompt.

Ruth Oh ... (*Peering at her closely*) Great heavens. So you are ... silly of me.

Val I think you're brilliant in this play.

Ruth Oh, thank you.

Val Very — er — convincing.

Ruth I have to be, duckie. The poor man depends on my brilliant — er — whatever to make his drivel meaningful. But one needs to be fortified, because one has a problem. We were professionals, you know. Worked with the big names. Credits above the title, dear — until I got my problem. Do you have a problem?

Val Er ... Well, er ...

Ruth Don't — that is my advice, don't have a problem. Problems are the very devil. Gordon has one.

Val Does he?

Ruth Yes — he thinks he's a playwright and he's married to me.

Val Oh.

Ruth Where is it all going to end? That's what I ask myself. I'm a fallen woman, Meg ——

Val Val.

Ruth (*maudlin, near to tears*) — a fallen woman, Val. A slave to the grape and a burden to my loved one ...

Sonia (*off, enraged*) My God! The dirty little bastard!

Val looks up, startled

Ruth Don't interrupt me, dear. I'm not worthy to gather up the crumbs under his table — or ... oh, dammit — could you get me a drink?

Sonia charges in, outraged

Sonia There is a disgusting little creep with a beard slinking about outside and making gestures at me through the dressing-room window. If I get my hands on him ... Oh, hallo, Ruth — where is everybody?

Ruth Lost ... lost ... we are all lost .... (*She rocks about with her head in her hands*)

Sonia Yes ... (*To Val*) Drunk, I suppose?

Val Well ...

Sonia Did you see him?

Val Who?

Sonia The bearded deviant. If the window hadn't been jammed I'd have jumped out and got him. Where's Gordon?

Val He went off and Stuart went after him.

Sonia Typical! When there's trouble about the men disappear.

Ruth He's left me, Sonia ... Gordon's left me. The fuse has finally blown. I criticized his masterpiece.

Sonia What masterpiece?

Ruth Falling down a well ... this one ... I told him it was twaddle — twaddle, twaddle. (*She falls into a boozy sleep*)

Sonia Well it is but this isn't the best time to tell him. I suppose he threw a tantrum.

Val Well — sort of ...

Sonia I'd better go and pacify him. This whole day has been a complete waste of time.

Val Stuart was going to do that.

Sonia Stuart? Stuart couldn't pacify a folded umbrella. (*Stopping by the exit*) Go and telephone the police.

Val Police?

Sonia Yes, they're supposed to apprehend sexual offenders.

Val But ...

Sonia But what?

Val Well ...

Sonia Look, the man's obviously an impostor; he's wearing a false beard.

Ruth I knew a man with a false beard once, thought he was Moses — poor fellow ... they certified him. (*She nods off*)

Val Are you absolutely certain? I mean he could be a thespian.

Sonia Oh, for goodness sake, do something positive.

Val Yes, yes, something — er — positive. Phone the police. Right.

Val scuttles off

Sonia God help us if we dry. She'll take ten minutes to find the cue.

Sonia goes

Ruth sleeps peacefully for a moment or two

Mr Brisket steals into the auditorium; he is carrying a case and wearing a beard. He is in late middle-age. He sees Ruth and goes up to the stage

Brisket I say — I say, excuse me. (*He gets no reaction. He climbs on to the stage*) I say? Mrs Partridge? (*Louder*) Hallo!

Ruth (*waking with a start*) Ahh! Go away! Go away! I'm not ready yet.

Brisket (*jumping back in alarm*) Oh ... I'm sorry — I'm so sorry ...

Ruth Who the devil are you?

Brisket Brisket.

Ruth Biscuit?

Brisket No, Brisket.

Ruth Do I know you?

Brisket Well ... er ...

Ruth You gave me one hell of a fright, luvvie. One hell of a fright. I thought you were the grim reaper.

Brisket Oh, hardly, hardly.

Ruth The beard, you see.

Brisket Oh — the beard.

Ruth And the scythe ...

Brisket I haven't got a scythe.

Ruth Nor you have ... no matter. (*Suspiciously*) Is it false?

Brisket Pardon?

Ruth The beard.

Brisket The beard?

Ruth That is what I said, are you deaf?

Brisket No.

Ruth Well, that's a comfort. You see, apparently there is a man with a false beard roaming about interfering with women.

Brisket Oh ... ah ... I do assure you, Mrs Partridge, that this beard is not false. It is entirely my own.

Ruth Well it looks false to me, it looks completely ... What did you call me?

Brisket Mrs Partridge ... You are Mrs Partridge. Er — from the Mothers Union?

Ruth (*thundering*) The Mothers Union, dear boy? Do I look as if I'm from the Mothers Union?

Brisket Well, no — on second thoughts, no. You are not Mrs Partridge?

Ruth I certainly am not!

Brisket This is most confusing. Perhaps she's the other lady?

Ruth What other lady?

Brisket The one I signalled to through the window.

Ruth I do hope, Mr Biscuit, that you do not make a habit of going about in a false beard like this signalling to ladies in windows.

Brisket Certainly not, madam, and my name is ——

Ruth I've been warned about you, Mr Biscuit. You'd better not try anything funny with me, I may be a little under the weather but I have a voice that can be heard at the back of the hall (*rearing up menacingly*) and by God I can scream like the very devil!

Brisket (*jumping back again*) No, madam, please. I do assure you my beard is not false. Look! Look! (*He tugs at his beard*) It is mine, madam. Mine. I am bona fide, madam. Bona fide ...

Ruth (*winding herself up*) I don't care who you are. You look
highly suspicious. A woman is not safe on her own these days. Not
safe anywhere. I know elderly women who daren't stick their
noses outside for fear of being ravished by men with false beards.
(*She gestures extravagantly*) What is this world coming to, Mr
Biscuit. When violence stalks the streets. Where are we going?
Where are we going? (*She crouches and sobs in a loud voice*) Is
there no end to it?

Brisket starts to flee

(*Thundering at him*) Come back.
Brisket (*brought up short*) But, madam ... I — er ..
Ruth Come back. (*Wailing*) Woe! Woe! Woe! (*She rocks about
beating her breasts*)
Brisket (*returning anxiously*) Er — are you all right? Perhaps
I ——
Ruth (*letting fly*) Begone! Begone! With your false beard and
sticky searching fingers. Hop it! Buzz off! (*Screaming with
marvellous projection*) Ahhhh!
Brisket (*leaping away*) No ... please, please ... steady on.
Ruth *Ahhhhhh!*
Brisket (*highly agitated*) My God! This is awful. Calm yourself,
madam. Calm yourself.
Ruth *Ahhhhhh!*
Brisket (*panicking*) Oh, where is Mrs Partridge? Mrs Partridge!
Mrs Partridge!

He rushes off straight into the arms of Sonia, who is returning

Sonia Get away from me! Filthy little beast!

*Sonia hurls him to the floor, where he lies prone, his case skidding
across the stage with a crash and tinkle*

Stuart, Gordon and Val enter

Stuart What the hell's going on? (*He sees Brisket on the floor*) Oh, my God! (*To Sonia*) Did you do this?

Sonia (*with satisfaction*) Yes.

Stuart (*going on his knees and attempting to revive Brisket, who appears to be out cold*) Isn't that carrying feminism a little far, Sonia. The man's unconscious.

Sonia He's a pervert. He came at me. I struck him in self-defence. He was attacking Ruth. Didn't you hear her screaming?

Stuart Of course I did. I should imagine the whole village heard her screaming.

Gordon (*trots across to Ruth*) Oh, poor Bunny ... poor Bunny.

Ruth appears to be entirely unruffled

Stuart (*smacking Mr Brisket's cheeks*) Wake up — wake up, Mr ... What's his name?

Ruth Biscuit.

Stuart Biscuit?

Ruth Biscuit, Biscuit ...

Gordon Calm down, Bunny — it's all over now.

Stuart Wake up, Mr Biscuit ...

Val (*moving down, anxiously*) I couldn't find a telephone. I'm terribly sorry. Oh dear, is he all right?

Stuart Of course he's not all right. He could be dead for all I know.

Val (*horrified*) Dead? Dead? Ahh! (*She faints on top of Stuart*)

Stuart Get her off me!

Sonia (*hurling Val aside*) If he's dead, it's his own fault. I simply pushed him in self-defence. The man's a pervert.

Brisket (*reviving partly*) Pills — pills ...

Stuart Didn't it occur to you, before you struck this man down, that he might, might just have been an innocent bystander?

Sonia No. Ruth was screaming.

Brisket (*gasping*) Pills — pills ...

Stuart Ruth screams for a pastime when she's drunk, you should know that.

Gordon Oh, I say. That's most unfair.

Brisket Pills — pills.

Stuart Come off it, Gordon. We all know that Ruth has a drink problem.

Gordon Possibly, but it does not have to be revealed to the entire company.

Brisket Pills.

Stuart (*to Sonia*) I suppose you imagine that all men are perverts.

Sonia Yes.

Brisket Pills — pills.

Stuart What? (*Peering at Brisket*) Oh God! He's going purple.

Val (*coming round*) Where am I?

Brisket Pills ...

Stuart Oh, pills ... where?

Brisket Pocket ...

Stuart Right. (*He rifles through his pockets*)

Val I must have fainted. (*She struggles to her feet*)

Stuart Christ! Look at him, it's a heart condition. If I can't find these pills, he'll probably die.

Val Die? Oh! ... (*She reels about*)

Sonia Pull yourself together, Val. Show some female guts for once.

Val I can't, it's psychosomatic ... Ahh! (*She falls down*)

Sonia Stupid woman!

Stuart Got them. Under the tongue?

Brisket Yes ...

Stuart Let's hope to God this works. (*To Sonia*) If this man is the adjudicator, we're in dead trouble.

Sonia Of course he's not the adjudicator. Adjudicators never arrive before the performance.

Stuart Some of them come early to look round.

Sonia Not this early. The man's a pervert.

Ruth His name's Biscuit. Does one recall any adjudicators by the name of Biscuit, Piglet?

Gordon No, Bunny.

Ruth Am I forgiven, Piglet?

Gordon Of course, Bunny — of course.

Ruth I have been through the valley of the shadow of death, Piglet. Set upon by men with false beards.

Gordon Awful, Bunny — awful. Take comfort Piglet's here.

Sonia (*sickened*) Oh, my God!

Mrs Partridge, a middle-aged lady, enters nervously through the auditorium armed with a hockey stick

Mrs Partridge Excuse me, have you booked this hall?
Gordon (*resuming control*) We are the WADS.
Mrs Partridge Pardon.
Gordon (*advancing to the edge of the stage*) WADS.
Mrs Partridge (*brandishing the stick*) Please don't come any closer. Why are all those people lying on the floor?
Ruth That one is a sexual pervert with a false beard. And that one is — the prompt.
Mrs Partridge (*utterly confused and nervous*) Oh, really?
Gordon I think you owe us an explanation.
Mrs Partridge Keep away.
Brisket (*recovering and seeing Mrs Partridge brandishing her stick*) Great heavens, another one ... (*He clutches at Stuart*) Don't leave me. These women are violent.
Gordon Are you on the committee?
Mrs Partridge (*swiping at him*) Keep your distance!
Gordon (*leaping back*) Good God!
Mrs Partridge I suggest you leave quietly. My husband has summoned the police.
Gordon Police?
Stuart Oh no ... (*He beats his forehead*) Kismet!
Gordon My God! I'm going to have a word with that committee. It's not good enough. They bring us to this godforsaken hut in some remote village and send in a sexual maniac who attacks my wife with a false beard and now this demented woman threatening us with a hockey stick. Who are you, madam? What is the big idea? And where is the management?
Mrs Partridge Don't think you can bluster your way out of this, my good man. You and your gang, breaking in here, fighting and screaming and shifting the furniture.
Gordon Is the woman mad?
Stuart No, Gordon, I fear not. I think we must be in the wrong place.

And that Sonia has typically jumped to the conclusion that Mr
Biscuit is a sexual deviant.

Brisket Brisket — the name's Brisket.

Mrs Partridge Brisket?

Brisket Brisket.

Mrs Partridge Are you Arnold Brisket of Lanes and Hedgerows?

Brisket Yes. Are you Mrs Partridge of the Mothers Union?

Mrs Partridge Yes.

Brisket The South Westbury Mothers Union?

Mrs Partridge Certainly. I have been expecting you, Mr Brisket,
in the vestry; we are assembled there.

Gordon (*utterly confused*) What is going on? Are they a comedy
turn?

Mrs Partridge I don't know who you people are; I have never
heard of WADS or whatever you call yourselves. But I must warn
you that my husband is the vicar of South Westbury and this is
church property and I intend to have you arrested.

Brisket (*staggering up*) Mrs Partridge, I have a serious complaint—

Stuart South Westbury? My God it is the wrong place. (*Hissing*)
Gordon — Gordon.

Brisket I have been violently assaulted, Mrs Partridge, by one of
your lady members and screamed at by another. I really think that
you owe me an explanation. (*With a manful effort and heavy
breathing and gasps he climbs into the auditorium*)

Stuart This is South Westbury Church Hall, Gordon. We're in a
king-sized cock-up — Gordon? Gordon? (*He sidles across to
Gordon*)

But Gordon is too confused to take anything in

Brisket (*labouring alarmingly*) I have an extremely precarious
heart condition, Mrs Partridge, and being flung to the floor by one
of your mothers could have been fatal——

Stuart We'd better do a runner before it's too late. I'm a govern-
ment employee. I have my reputation to think of.

Stuart creeps off

Brisket — and if it hadn't been for this kind gentleman here, er ... (*He indicates the now empty space where he last saw Stuart*) ... well, if it hadn't been for the kind gentleman I would have been a gonner. Ah. (*He produces a hanky and mops his brow*)

Mrs Partridge These people are not members of the Mothers Union, Mr Brisket. I'm having them arrested. Hadn't you better sit down?

Gordon What are they talking about? How did the Mothers Union get into this?

Ruth Poor man has a fixation, Bunny. He seemed to imagine that I was one.

Stuart pokes his head round the curtain

Stuart Come on! Come on! The situation is highly volatile! Sonia!

Sonia (*still smouldering*) What?

Stuart (*gesturing*) Come on for God's sake. You could be facing ten years!

Sonia It was self-defence, the man's a pervert. Hey!

Stuart grabs her

Oh God! *Men!*

Stuart yanks her off

Brisket (*recovering slightly*) Moreover, Mrs Partridge, I fear I shall be unable to exhibit my slides of rural paths and hedgerows as arranged.

Stuart hisses and gestures from the wings

Gordon (*still dithering about on stage*) I don't understand what's happening.

Ruth I think we are all going to the pub, Piglet.

Brisket I shall not — on account of equipment being undoubtedly — damaged — and — and I shall not ... Ah! Ah!

He gasps, sways and clutches Mrs Partridge, who drops her stick

Mrs Partridge Oh! ... Oh!

They sway about precariously

Gordon (*completely confused*) This is ridiculous. Why is he dancing with her? Are they next on?
Ruth (*soothing*) Come along, Piglet ... come along.

Ruth leads Gordon out gently

Brisket Pill! Pill! (*He clutches Mrs Partridge in urgent despair*)
Mrs Partridge (*in a strangled voice*) Please, Mr Brisket — you have me by the throat ...
Brisket Pill!
Mrs Partridge Mr Brisket!
Brisket Pill!
Mrs Partridge (*struggling with him towards the exit*) Yes, we will see to your needs in the vestry, Mr Brisket, the ladies have prepared tea. But would you kindly remove your hand from my throat — you are throttling me.
Brisket (*weakly*) Pill ...
Mrs Partridge It's just across the graveyard. You'll be safer there — Mr Brisket, please ...

Brisket and Mrs Partridge go out

Val (*surfacing*) Where am I? (*She staggers to her feet*) I must have fainted.
Stuart (*off*) Hell's teeth!
Val What?

Stuart peers round the border curtain

Stuart Val — come on — the police are coming.

Val Police?

Stuart They've called the police.

Val Oh— er — police?

Stuart If you stay here they'll arrest you. Come on!

Val (*panicking*) Arrest me? Arrest me? What for? What for? Not — not for Mr Biscuit ... What's happened to Mr Biscuit? Oh God! Oh ... (*She starts to faint*)

Stuart (*urgently*) No, Val — no!

Val Ahhh! (*She faints*)

Stuart Damn and blast! (*He scuttles on*) Wake up! Wake up! (*He smacks her face but to no avail*)

Gordon (*in high agitation, off*) But, Constable there has been a mistake, I tell you. We are a well-known drama group — we are the WADS — the WADS. We are presenting a world première in this festival here. A world première. You can't arrest us — I don't understand — I am completely confused. What is going on? Will somebody tell me what is going on? We're supposed to be having a technical rehearsal. (*He fades away protesting*)

Stuart Nicked by the Mothers Union. What a shambles. I give up. (*He rises and grabs Val by the wrists*) Well, there's one thing I'm pretty certain about. This is the last time I get mixed up in a world première with this mob. I am definitely joining the operatic.

Stuart goes dragging Val behind him as ——

——the CURTAIN *falls*

FURNITURE AND PROPERTY LIST

On stage: Nil

Off stage: Plastic shopping bag (**Val**)
                Two chairs (**Val**)
                Large throne-like chair (**Val**)
                Battered settee (**Val**)
                Chair (**Gordon**)
                Case (**Mr Brisket**)
                Hockey stick (**Mrs Partridge**)

Personal: **Gordon**: crumpled bit of paper in pocket
                Stuart: script
                Mr Brisket: handkerchief and bottle of pills in pocket

LIGHTING PLOT

Property fittings required: nil
Interior. The same scene throughout

To open: Black-out

| *Cue* 1: | When ready | (Page 1) |
| | *Shaft of light off* L | |

| *Cue* 2 | **Val**: "Er ..." | (Page 2) |
| | *Bring up full general lighting* | |

EFFECTS PLOT

Cue 1 **Val**: "Oh, heavens!"   (Page 9)
Thump, clatter

Cue 2 **Mr Brisket**'s case skids across the stage   (Page 20)
Crash, tinkle